Renaissance Dance Music for Guitar Ensemble

MB99954

by *Alan Hirsh*

**Free Guitar Parts II, III, IV, V and optional percussion parts
are available online as a download!**
Visit: www.melbay.com/99954

© 2010 BY MEL BAY PUBLICATIONS, INC., PACIFIC, MO 63069.
ALL RIGHTS RESERVED. INTERNATIONAL COPYRIGHT SECURED. B.M.I. MADE AND PRINTED IN U.S.A.
No part of this publication may be reproduced in whole or in part, or stored in a retrieval system, or transmitted in any form
or by any means, electronic, mechanical, photocopy, recording, or otherwise, without written permission of the publisher.

Visit us on the Web at www.melbay.com or billsmusicshelf.com

Table of Contents

Renaissance Suite I
Anonymous

I. Saltarello

II. Pavane

III. Ungaresca

IV. Saltarello

Notes

The arrangements in this collection are designed for a large guitar ensemble (guitar orchestra). Though it is desirable to perform them with multiple guitars to a part, one guitar to a part works satisfactorily. Where divisi is marked over a staff, the part divides for two groups of players (e.g. one group of players plays an upper part and the other group of players plays the lower part).

All of the arrangements are in five parts and are organized as follows:

Guitar I is the hardest.
Guitar III is the easiest.
Guitar II, IV, and V (low D) are intermediate.

Renaissance Dance Suite I
I. Saltarello

Arranged by Alan Hirish

Anonymous

II. Pavana

III. Ungaresca

div.

tap soundboard with thumb

unis.

IV. Saltarello

w/ flesh

Tambura

Tambura

Tambura

Tambura

Renaissance Suite II
Anonymous

I. Tarantella

II. Pavane

III. Spagna Contrapunta

Renaissance Dance Suite II
I. Tarantella

Arranged by Alan Hirsh

Anonymous

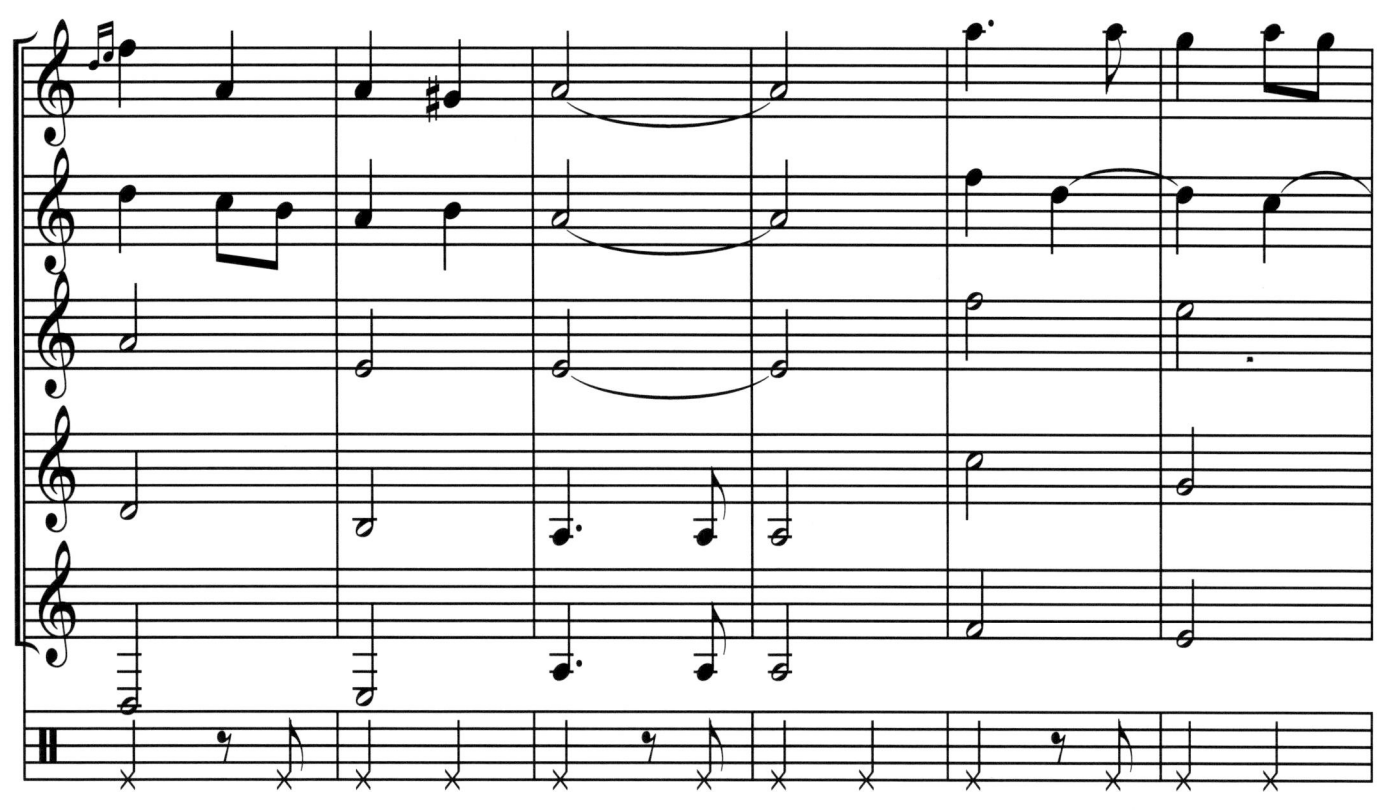

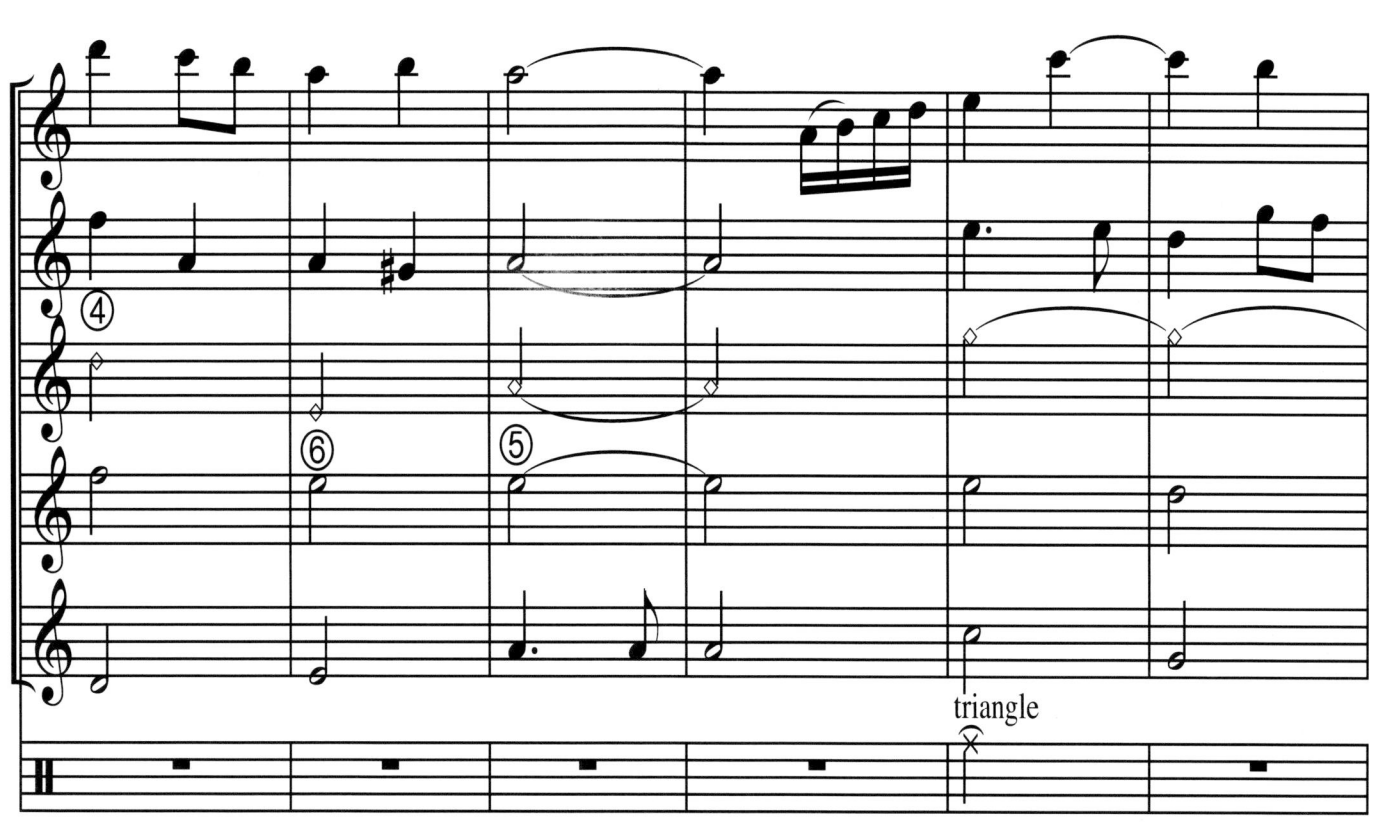

triangle

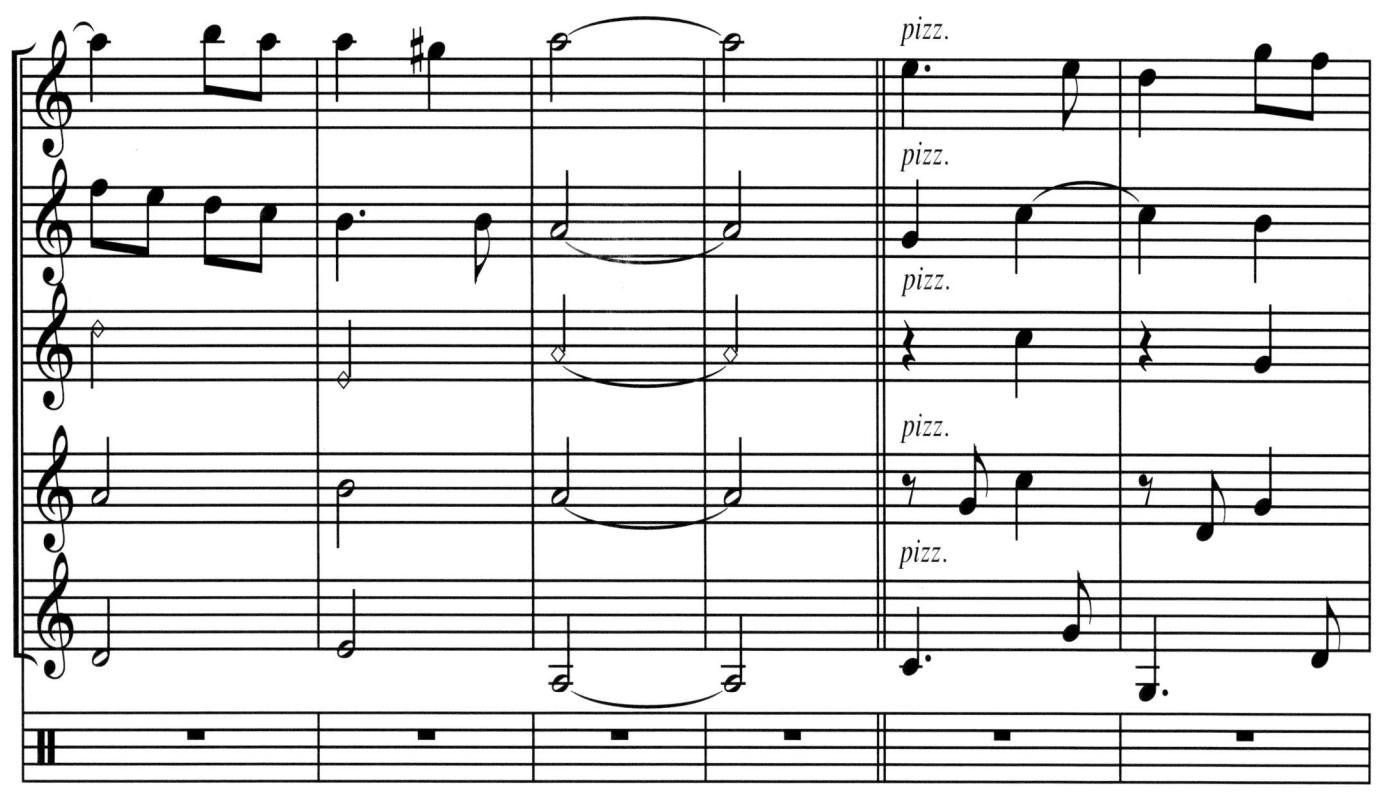

II. Pavana

38

III. Spagna Contrapunto

Francesco Canova da Milano

Pos. II

Dances from "Dansereye"
Tielman Susato

Score with optional percussion

I. Bergeret sans roch and Reprise

II. Pavane Mille regretz

III. Ronde

Three Dances from Dansereye
I. Bergeret sans roch & Reprise

Arranged by Alan Hirsh

Tielman Susato

II. Pavane Mille regretz

III. Ronde

61

GUITAR I

Renaissance Dance

Arranged by Alan Hirsh

I. Saltarello
II. Pavana
III. Ungaresca
IV. Saltarello

Renaissance Dance Suite I
I. Saltarello

Guitar I

Arranged by Alan Hirsh

Anonymous

II. Pavana

III. Ungaresca

IV. Saltarello

GUITAR I

Renaissance Dance Suite II

Arranged by Alan Hirsh

I. Tarantella
II. Pavane
III. Spagna Contrapunto

Renaissance Dance Suite II
I. Tarantella

Guitar I

Arranged by Alan Hirsh

Anonymous

II. Pavana

III. Spagna Contrapunto

Francesco Canova da Milano

Guitar I

Three Dances from "Dansereye"

By Tielman Susato
Arranged by Alan Hirsh

I. Bergeret sans roch & Reprise

II. Pavane Mille regretz

III. Ronde

Three Dances from Dansereye
I. Bergeret sans roch & Reprise

Guitar I

Arranged by Alan Hirsh

Tielman Susato

II. Pavane Mille regretz

III. Ronde

UNIQUELY INTERESTING MUSIC!